■ SCHOLASTIC

GRADE 5

50+ Super-Fun Math Activities

by Joseph D'Agnese

NEW YORK • TORONTO • LONDON • AUCKLAND • SYDNEY
MEXICO CITY • NEW DELHI • HONG KONG • BUENOS AIRES

Teaching Resources

Edited by Jean Liccione

Cover design by Ka-Yeon Kim-Li

Interior design by Ellen Matlach Hassell for Boultinghouse & Boultinghouse, Inc.

Interior illustrations by Maxie Chambliss and Manuel Rivera

ISBN-13: 978-0-545-20820-8

ISBN-10: 0-545-20820-3

Contents

(continued on the next page)

✳ This activity includes a reproducible.

✳ This activity includes a reproducible.

Introduction

Welcome to *50+ Super-Fun Math Activities Grade 5*. This book contains a unique collection of activities that reinforce important first-grade-level mathematics concepts and skills and support the math standards recommended by the National Council of Teachers of Mathematics (NCTM). See page 6, for more.

The book is organized by nine major content topics. When you're teaching a particular math concept or skill, just check the Contents page. Browse the activities listed under each topic to find just the right one to reinforce students' learning. Each major topic has projects, games, activities, and ready-to-use reproducibles designed to reinforce specific learning objectives. The activities will also get students interested and excited, and encourage them to value math and become confident mathematicians.

ACTIVITY FEATURES

The activities include grouping suggestions, lists of needed materials, teaching tips, step-by-step directions, and easy Assessment ideas. Some activities also include the following features:

◆ Extensions and Variations—ideas for taking the math skills and concepts further

◆ Home Links—quick and easy activities students can do at home with their families

◆ Writing Connections—suggestions for encouraging students to communicate and reinforce what they've learned through writing.

ABOUT GROUPING

Sometimes it's important for students to work together in groups or pairs, to collaborate and communicate. Sometimes they need to work independently. The activities in this book support a variety of needs, from independent to whole class work. You'll find a grouping suggestion at the beginning of each activity.

ASSESSING STUDENTS' WORK

NCTM recommends a variety of approaches to assessment of the various dimensions of a student's mathematical learning. The following assessment suggestions are incorporated throughout this book:

◆ ideas for group and class discussion

◆ ideas for journal writing and written response

◆ ideas for ongoing informal teacher observations

On pages 61–63, you'll also find suggested ways of observing and keeping records of students' work as well as a reproducible student Self-Evaluation Form and an Assessment Checklist and Scoring Rubric.

Remember that you can review students' self-assessments and their journals and written responses to see not only how well they understand concepts but also how well they express their mathematical understandings.

CONNECTIONS TO THE MATH STANDARDS

The activities in this book are designed to support you in meeting the following process standards for students in grades 3–5 recommended by the National Council of Teachers of Mathematics (NCTM):

Problem Solving The activities promote a problem-solving approach to learning. Throughout the book, you'll find suggestions for encouraging students to develop, apply, and explain their problem-solving strategies.

Reasoning & Proof Suggestions in the last step of each activity can serve as prompts to help students draw logical conclusions, explain and justify their thinking, and "pull it together" to make sense of the mathematics skills and concepts they've just used. Activities encourage students to use patterns and relationships as they work.

Communication Activities include ideas for helping students organize and consolidate their mathematical thinking through class discussions and writing connections.

Connections Activities tie to the real world, to the interests of fifth-grade students, and to other areas of the curriculum. The purpose of many activities is to bridge conceptual and procedural knowledge, and to bridge different topics in mathematics.

Representation Students use manipulatives, pictures and diagrams, and numerical representations to complete the activities.

The grids below show how the activities correlate to the other math standards for grades 3–5.

PAGE	Number & Operations	Algebra	Geometry	Measurement	Data Analysis & Probability
8	◆	◆			
10	◆	◆			
12	◆				
14	◆				
16	◆				
17	◆				
19	◆				
21	◆				
23	◆				
24	◆				
25	◆				
27	◆				
28	◆				
30	◆	◆	◆		

PAGE	Number & Operations	Algebra	Geometry	Measurement	Data Analysis & Probability
32			◆		
34	◆			◆	◆
35	◆			◆	
36					
38	◆	◆			
39	◆	◆			
40	◆				
42	◆			◆	
43	◆				
45	◆				
47	◆				◆
48					◆
49					◆
50					◆

PAGE	Number & Operations	Algebra	Geometry	Measurement	Data Analysis & Probability
51					◆
53					◆
55	◆			◆	
57	◆			◆	◆
59	◆				
60	◆	◆	◆		

Source: National Council of Teachers of Mathematics. (2000). *Principles and standards for school mathematics.* Reston: VA: NCTM. www.nctm.org

Any Time Is Math Time

Use these quick activities any time you have a few minutes to fill.

1. **Wanna Date?** Ask students to name today's date. Then ask a volunteer to name something mathematical about today's date. For example:

   ◆ March 13: 13 is a prime number. If you double it, you get 26, which isn't.

   ◆ September 30: 30's factors are 1, 2, 3, 5, 6, 15, and 30.

2. **Math in Your Shoes** Ask students look at their shoes and the shoes of their classmates. Tell them you'd like to know something about the class—but you want you get your information in the form of fractions. For example: What fraction of students in the class are wearing sneakers? What fraction of students in the class are wearing shoes with red in them?

3. **Time To Pick Me!** This is a good exercise when you need to choose a student to do a popular task. Tell students that you want them to close their eyes and raise their hands when they think one minute has passed. Suggest that they count quietly to themselves to help judge the time. Keep track with a watch and choose the person whose hand goes up at the correct time.

4. **Measurement Q and A** Keep a yardstick or meterstick prominently displayed in the classroom. When you're in the hallways of the school, ask students how many yards (meters) long various distances are. (You can even assign students to use the yardstick and find the actual distances.)

5. **Equation Telephone** Play the game Telephone—with a twist! Whisper a math equation in the ear of the first student. For example: "6 x 7, pass it on!" Ask each student in turn to pass the equation down the line to the last student. Ask the last student to say what the equation is—and to announce the answer. Then reveal the original problem.

6. **Number Partners** Here's a good way to get students to choose partners quickly. Tell students that they will count off to receive a number. Ask them to remember what their own number is—as well as everyone else's! Have students count off: The first student is 1, the second is 2, and so on. Challenge students to pick a partner whose number, when added to theirs, creates the lowest possible sum.

7. **The Coins in My Pocket . . .** While students are waiting in line, try this mental math money activity: Announce that you have a certain amount of money in your pocket, say, $1.32. Tell them that all of the money is change. Can they guess the combination of coins? In order to figure it out, allow students to ask you yes or no questions. For example: Are there any quarters? Do have three dimes?

8. **Pattern Count-Off** Tell students that you are going to create a number pattern. Stress that students must remember the numbers they are given. Give a pattern such as 1, 2, 2, 3, 3, 3, 4, 4, 4, 4, 5, 5, 5, 5, 5, etc. Invite the class to figure out the pattern. The winner gets to invent the next pattern.

Grouping

Pairs

You'll Need

For each pair:

◆ **Patterns Please! (reproducible page 9)**

◆ 30–50 counters

Teaching Tip

If you have fewer counters, have students work in larger groups. If you have more counters, students can work individually.

Patterns, Please!

This board activity allows students to discover the patterns inherent in numbers from 1 to 100.

PREPARATION

Set aside an area in the classroom where students can grab a handful of counters and still go back for more.

DIRECTIONS

1. Explain to students that numbers have attributes, or things in common, which can be explored on a hundred chart, reproducible page 9. As an example, you might write these numbers on the chalkboard:

    5 10 15 20 25 30 35 40

    Ask students to explain the traits the numbers have in common.

2. Now ask students to find these numbers on their hundred chart. Let them use their counters to cover the numbers. Ask students if they can continue the series and whether the counters form a pattern or shape.

3. Here are some other number patterns students can look for: multiples of 3, 4, 5, 6, 7, 8, 9, 10, 11, 12; factors of 90, 100; all even numbers; all odd numbers; all prime numbers; all numbers with 6 in them; all numbers with 2 or 7 in the ones place. Give students some examples to get them started, but encourage them to find number patterns and visual patterns of their own.

ASSESSMENT

Be sure that students are not covering numbers just because other groups are, or because their partners have instructed them to. In most instances, the counters will form a pattern. (Note: Prime numbers do not form a pattern.)

➤➤➤ EXTENSIONS

◆ Ask students to make a diagonal line (or X or square) on their boards. Then ask students to describe something interesting about the numbers they covered.

◆ Allow students to come up with their own attributes to search for and cover.

Patterns, Please!

1	2	3	4	5	6	7	8	9	10
11	12	13	14	15	16	17	18	19	20
21	22	23	24	25	26	27	28	29	30
31	32	33	34	35	36	37	38	39	40
41	42	43	44	45	46	47	48	49	50
51	52	53	54	55	56	57	58	59	60
61	62	63	64	65	66	67	68	69	70
71	72	73	74	75	76	77	78	79	80
81	82	83	84	85	86	87	88	89	90
91	92	93	94	95	96	97	98	99	100

Place-Value Vittles

Hungry for a big barbecue—and big numbers? This cookout game will help students with place value and regrouping.

Grouping

Small groups

You'll Need

◆ **Place-Value Vittles (reproducible page 11),** two copies for each group
◆ Paper
◆ Pencils
◆ Glue
◆ Paper clips

Writing Connection

Have students write a silly story about a cook who makes place-value shish kebabs of unusual foods. As an element of the story, they can provide pictures to show how the cook regroups when the number of ones, tens, hundreds, or thousands is greater than 9.

DIRECTIONS

1. It's time for a cookout. Explain to students that each group will work together to make one plate of place-value barbecue. Distribute reproducible page 11 and have students cut out the barbecue counters. They should make separate piles for ones, tens, hundreds, etc.

2. Demonstrate how to spin a paper clip around the point of a pencil placed at the center of the spinner. Each group spins to select a batch of vittles and then takes counters from their piles of vittles to make the number they spun. Tell them to do this four times. After each spin, have students add the new number to the previous sum by taking more place-value vittles. For example, if a group spins 3 hundreds, 12 ones, they can take these place value counters to represent their spin:

3. If the spin or the sum has more than 9 in a place, students must trade to put 10 together. (Example: 12 ones = 1 ten and 2 ones.)

4. After the last of four spins, the group should represent the final sum by pasting down the number of ten thousands, thousands, hundreds, tens, and ones and writing the number. Ask a representative from each group to read the final number and show the "plate" of barbecue they've made. Ask the rest of the class to determine whether the number is written correctly.

ASSESSMENT

Observe students as they work. Are they able to regroup across tens, hundreds, thousands? If they are having trouble, ask students to use only tens, hundreds, or thousands.

▶▶▶ EXTENSION

Ask students to design their own spinners and barbecue foods for place-value practice into the hundred thousands and the millions place.

Place-Value Vittles

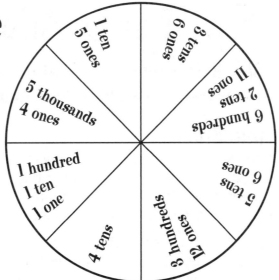

Ones	Tens	Hundreds	Thousands	Ten Thousands
Ones	Tens	Hundreds	Thousands	Ten Thousands
Ones	Tens	Hundreds	Thousands	Ten Thousands
Ones	Tens	Hundreds	Thousands	Ten Thousands
Ones	Tens	Hundreds	Thousands	Ten Thousands
Ones	Tens	Hundreds	Thousands	Ten Thousands

Eat 'Em & Add 'Em Diner

Chef Big Vic flips burgers at the Eat 'Em & Add 'Em Diner. His math is shaky, so your students can help him add.

DIRECTIONS

1. Explain the problem: Chef Big Vic is so busy flipping burgers at the Eat 'Em & Add 'Em Diner that he frequently does the math on people's guest checks incorrectly. Students' job is to find Big Vic's errors and rewrite the amount owed correctly.

2. Distribute reproducible page 13. Ask students to look at the menu board for prices at the diner. For each guest check, students should circle any incorrect charges, substitute the correct ones, and then calculate the correct totals.

ASSESSMENT

Answers: guest check 1: $7.15; guest check 2: $6.90, guest check 3: $11.20. If there are errors in students' work, try to ascertain if the student is having trouble doing the addition or finding the correct information on the menu.

⇥⇥⇥ EXTENSION

Share some menus from local diners with students. Ask them to compare prices for some typical breakfast foods. Ask students which diner they would go to and why. Ask them to consider things like which diner offers the best deal.

✛✛✛ VARIATION

Have students make their own selections from the Menu Board and then find the total amount they would spend. Pairs of students can exchange selections and check the addition.

Grouping

Individual

You'll Need

For each student:

◆ **Eat 'Em & Add 'Em Diner (reproducible page 13)**

◆ Paper

◆ Pencil

WELCOME TO THE
Eat 'Em & Add 'Em Diner

MENU

DRINKS .... SMALL ... LARGE
LEMON JUICE .... $.45 ... $.60
TOMATO SODA POP .... $.50 .... $.65
PEANUT BUTTER MALTED ...... $.90 ... $1.05
DIET PEANUT BUTTER MALTED .. $.80 .... $.95
CHOCOLATE WATER .... $.10 .... $.25
SALES TAX INCLUDED

BURGERS
PLAIN BURGER $3.00
TOPPINGS
PICKLES .... $.30
CHEWING GUM .... $.30
CHOCOLATE CHIPS .... $.35
TUNA FISH CHUNKS .... $.55
EXTRA CHEESE .... NO CHARGE
SALES TAX INCLUDED

Help these people out of a lunchtime mess by fixing their guest checks. First, circle the incorrect prices. Then rewrite the check with the correct prices. Figure out the correct totals and write them on the blanks.

GUEST CHECK 1

1 burger	$3.00
with pickles	$.30
2nd burger	$1.05
with chocolate chips	$.45
small tomato soda	$.65
Total	$5.45

Correct Total _____

GUEST CHECK 2

1 burger	$3.00
with chocolate chips	$.30
2nd burger	$3.70
with pickles	$.45
large chocolate water	$.25
Total	$5.45

Correct Total _____

GUEST CHECK 3

1 burger	$2.60
with pickles	$.20
2nd burger	$3.00
with gum	$.45
tuna chunks	$.65
3rd burger	$3.00
extra cheese	$1.00
large peanut	
butter malted	$.80
Total	$11.70

Correct Total _____

Big Numbers on Planet Frooze

As they plot their course to Planet Frooze, students work with HUGE numbers in story problems.

DIRECTIONS

1. Review basic ideas about adding and subtracting large numbers. Students' work will be more successful if they remember to align numbers correctly when they write out their problems. Ones, tens, hundreds, and so on must align.

2. Distribute reproducible page 15 and ask students to complete it independently.

3. When students are finished, discuss their work. If students' answers vary, ask a volunteer to show the computation on the chalkboard. You might then have another student use the calculator as a second means of verification.

ASSESSMENT

Answers: 1. 1,567,734 freebs **2.** 37,201,409 gleebs **3.** 12,325,379 Froozians **4.** She runs 47,862 more vomils than snorts. (134,607 vomils – 86,745 snorts) **5.** 10,363,579 fruits in all.

➔➔➔ EXTENSION

Explain to students that the problems they encountered on the way to Planet Frooze are actually more difficult than many real-life addition problems. Ask them to write one word problem using "real" numbers and facts they find in a local news story.

Grouping

Individual

You'll Need

For each student:

◆ **Big Numbers on Planet Frooze (reproducible page 15)**

◆ Pencil

◆ Paper

◆ Calculator (optional)

Writing Connection

Students might enjoy writing a math story about their adventures as a stowaway aboard a spaceship bound for Planet Frooze. Ask them to include math problems encountered along the way.

Big Numbers on Planet Frooze

Read these word problems. You will need to work with big numbers to find the solutions. Are you ready? Blast off!

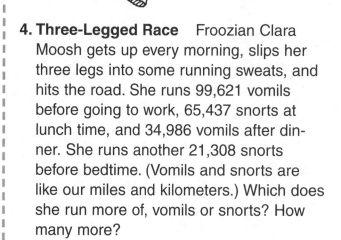

1. Space Dough   Claptrack Norsbott, commander of Planet Frooze's Space Fleet, loves fast food. She orders her crew to dock the spaceship at the Hover-Thru window of Froozle's restaurant. She spends 1,478,432 freebs (that's the money on Frooze) on a Galaxy Burger, 68,835 freebs on a Weightless Shake, and 20,467 freebs on a Frapple Pie. How many freebs did Commander Norsbott spend in all?

Answer: _____

2. Gleeb Guzzler   They don't use gallons on Frooze–they use gleebs. On Earth we fill our cars with gas. On Frooze they use papaya juice. Malmar Vorton scoots into a service station and asks for a complete fill-up. The attendant squeezes out 34,214,003 gleebs of juice into his scooter tank, 2,987,406 gleebs into his reserve tank, and fills Vorton's thermos with 2,300,002 gleebs of papaya juice. How many gleebs of juice did Malmar get for his scooter?

Answer: _____

3. Stadium Stuffer   For the Frooze Olympics, Bulbus Stadium is packed with 12,460,301 beings—many of them from neighboring galaxies. Exactly 42,320 Nootlians are here from the gassy planet, Nootlia. From Thrummta come 62,401 horn-faced Thrummtans. And from Vomrole are exactly 30,201 Vomrolites. The rest of the people are all Froozians. How many Froozians is that?

Answer: _____

4. Three-Legged Race   Froozian Clara Moosh gets up every morning, slips her three legs into some running sweats, and hits the road. She runs 99,621 vomils before going to work, 65,437 snorts at lunch time, and 34,986 vomils after dinner. She runs another 21,308 snorts before bedtime. (Vomils and snorts are like our miles and kilometers.) Which does she run more of, vomils or snorts? How many more?

Answer: _____

5. Froozie Smoothies   Commander Norsbott and her kids like to whip up a fruity dessert. They get out their Mega-Blender and toss in 3,490,637 strawberries, 5,622,942 bananas, and 2,500,000 mangoes. The Commander's son, Waldo, yells, "Not so many mangoes! They are way too fruity!" So the Commander removes half of the mangoes before switching on the blender. How many pieces of fruit do they end up using to make their Froozies?

Answer: _____

6. Make up your own big-number problem about the Planet Frooze. Ask a classmate to solve it. (Be sure you know the answer.)

Batter Up! Subtraction

In this classroom version of baseball, students practice subtracting with zeros.

Grouping

Two teams

You'll Need

◆ Scorekeeper
◆ Calculator (optional)

Teaching Tip

You might want to act as umpire, and decide ahead of time how many digits the largest numbers will be.

PREPARATION

Select four spots in the classroom to be first, second, and third bases, and home plate. Draw a scoreboard on the chalkboard or on chart paper with seven innings and space to record runs for two teams.

DIRECTIONS

1. Warm up by discussing strategies for subtracting from numbers that have zeros. Ask students for their ideas. For example, when subtracting from a number with more than one zero, regroup more than one place at a time.

$$
\begin{array}{r}
1\ 1\ 9\ 10 \\
\cancel{1200} \\
-\ 1186 \\
\hline
14
\end{array}
\begin{array}{l}
\rightarrow 119 \text{ tens and } 10 \text{ ones} \\
\rightarrow 118 \text{ tens and } 6 \text{ ones} \\
\rightarrow \ \ 1 \text{ ten and } \ \ 4 \text{ ones}
\end{array}
$$

2. Divide the class into two teams and explain the rules. The game is played like baseball, with three bases and home plate. At the beginning of an inning, a team sends a batter up with a number the team has chosen. The batter announces what his or her number is. The other team pitches a larger number ending with zeros at the batter. The batter must subtract his or her number from the number pitched. If the batter completes the problem correctly, he or she advances one base. For example:

   A batter steps up to plate. She announces the number 1,984. The other team pitches the number 4,000. The batter does the problem 4,000 – 1,984. If her answer is correct, she advances to first base. If she is incorrect, the batter is out. After three outs, the sides change.

3. The game is over after seven innings and there is a clear winner. If not, go into "extra innings" until one team scores.

ASSESSMENT

As students work at the chalkboard, observe their strategies. If an interesting technique for subtraction emerges, ask the student to explain his or her thinking to the class.

✦✦✦ VARIATION

The baseball game format can be used to build nearly any math skill. For instance, students can pitch numbers and ask the batter to tell whether the number is a prime, calculate a greatest common factor, tell which fraction is greater, perform a division problem, and so on.

Big Business Checkup

As students buy and sell their own "merchandise," they use their knowledge of adding and subtracting money.

DIRECTIONS

1. Divide the class into small groups. Explain that each group will be a business that buys and sells merchandise. Each business starts with $1,000,000 in their bank account.

2. Distribute the materials and ask groups to look through the magazines, clipping out pictures of items they'd like to sell: cars, toys, vacations, food, etc. Ask each group to choose five items related to their business. Have them tape or glue each item to a piece of paper or cardboard.

3. Ask students to assign a price to each item. Set a price range, say, $500 to $1,000,000. (Prices do not have to be realistic.) Ask them to label each item with its price.

4. Distribute several copies of reproducible page 18 to each group. Review the elements of a check and show students how to record their checks and money remaining in account on their check registers. Have one group at a time examine the merchandise of all the other groups. If the group wants to buy something, they can write a check to the other business.

5. Have students fill out their checkbook registers as a record of the items they bought, the amount spent, and the amount they have left. Groups should write individual checks for each item they buy so they can easily track the amounts spent and remaining.

6. At the end of the sale, ask each group to report on what they bought, why they bought it, and how much money they have left over. Discuss as a class the benefits of setting fair prices and the drawback of setting high or low ones. *(If your prices are too low, you end up selling everything and making little money. If they're too high, no one wants to buy the items.)*

ASSESSMENT

This is an excellent opportunity to see how students work together in groups. Check to see who is leading each group, who is keeping notes, who is being most vocal about purchases.

Grouping

Small groups

You'll Need

- **Big Business Checkup (reproducible page 18),** several copies for each group
- Paper
- Pencils
- Old magazines
- Scissors
- Paper or cardboard
- Tape or glue

Teaching Tip

You may want to make a rule that students buy at least one item from each of the other groups.

Big Business Check-Up

CHECKBOOK REGISTER OF:				BALANCE FORWARD
CHECK NO.	DATE	ISSUED TO/FOR	AMOUNT	RECORD STARTING AMOUNT HERE

NAME OF BUSINESS _____

ADDRESS _____

CITY/STATE _____

Check no. _____

Date _____ *19* ____

Pay to the order of _____ $ _____

_____ *Dollars*

BANK OF OUR CLASSROOM
1776 INDEPENDENCE, ANYTOWN, ANYPLACE

For _____

⑊1234567890⑊⑊2468013579⑊   SIGNATURE _____

Math Swamp

As they navigate around the dangerous math swamp, students practice muliplication, addition, and subtraction.

DIRECTIONS

1. Distribute reproducible page 20. Explain that the object of the activity is to go from one end of the swamp to the other. Students will connect the numbers and signs (x, +, −) to form correct math problems. If the path they've chosen is correct, the answer to one problem becomes the beginning number in the next. For example, 4 x 8 = 32 + 1 = 33 and so on. Remind students that the swamp is a kind of maze, so they might start out on a path and eventually come to a connection that doesn't work.

2. Give everyone time to get from START to END. Then discuss students' work. Have several students show the paths they followed. Was more than one path possible?

ASSESSMENT

Check that students have reached the swamp FINISH, so that the final math problem they solve results in a solution of zero. You might ask students who finish their work early to check each other's work to compare paths through the swamp. **Answer:** see path shown.

→→→ EXTENSION

Challenge students to create their own swamp mazes. All they need is some large grid paper. First they need to plot out a long math problem that snakes through the maze. Any remaining blanks should be filled in with "dummy" numbers or signs. (Mazes should be tested a few times before being considered finished.)

Mulitplication

Grouping
Individual

You'll Need

For each student:
◆ Math Swamp (reproducible page 20)
◆ Pencil

Math Swamp

START 3

−	162	=	54	X	4	=	12	X	5	=	60	−
56			9			6			52			
=			=			=			=			
107			27			72			2			
−	82	=	3	X	70	=	2	−	304	=	178	−
15			23			614			210			
=			=			=			=			
67			1,610			43			440			
X	17	=	1,140	−	556	=	1,054	X	13	=	342	−
15			620			2			390			
=			=			=			=			
1,006			990			2,108			52			
−	1,149	=	3	X	383	=	1,725	−	304	=	22	
1,103			210			562			11			
=			=			=			=			
46			415			1,546			41			
X	11	=	506	−	452	=	54	−	53	=	20	X

54
=
0 END

Get Buzz-y Multiplication

As they buzz through a multiplication hive, student "bees" beat their opponents by amassing a honey of a number!

DIRECTIONS

1. Distribute reproducible page 22. Explain to students that they'll play this game in pairs. The object of the game is to reach the opposite side of the beehive first—but with the most honey!

2. To start the game, students place one "bee" (or counter) on any START space on their side of the board. There are seven possible starting points on each side.

3. At each turn, players can move one space in any direction. They multiply the number of gallons of honey on the space they move to by the number in the space they previously occupied. (To begin the game, players multiply the first number they move to by 1.) They keep track of the number of gallons they accumulate on sheets of paper.

4. When a player's bee lands on a hexagon, the honey is gone! The student draws an X through that hexagon when the bee is moved out of it. No player may land there again. Two players may not occupy the same hexagon.

5. The player who is first to reach the END on the opposite side, with the greatest number of gallons of honey, is the winner.

6. Have students play three rounds of the game. Ask the class if they got better as they played the game. What trade-offs did they have to make? What strategies did they use?

ASSESSMENT

Note students' ability to do the multiplication correctly. Observe their strategies: Students should understand that moving to larger numbers and more numbers will get them more honey, but if they meander too often the other player may reach the end first and have more honey.

➔➔➔ EXTENSION

For division practice, assign a large number (such as 9,754 gallons) to each student. Have partners play the game, this time dividing as they go. The goal is to reach the opposite side with the least amount of honey. Students can simply discard any remainders and continue, using whole numbers.

Grouping

Pairs

You'll Need

For each pair:

◆ **Get Buzz-y (reproducible page 22),** three copies for each pair

◆ Two different-color counters

◆ Scrap paper

◆ Pencils

Writing Connection

Have students write a review of the game. What's fun about it? What's tricky about it? What advice would they give other students playing the game?

Name

Get Buzz-y Multiplication

Factor Face-Off

In this multiplication game, students work in teams to solve multiplication problems and score points.

PREPARATION

Make a list of 30–40 numbers students should know how to factor. Depending on the ability of the class, these can be numbers as simple as 10, 16, and 24, or as difficult as 81, 121, and 144.

DIRECTIONS

1. Review the concept of factor pairs: two numbers that, when multiplied, give a specified product. Use the number 12 as an example. Ask students to list all the factor pairs. *(1 x 12; 12 x 1; 2 x 6; 6 x 2; 3 x 4; 4 x 3)*

2. Ask students to form two teams. Set up two rows of seats facing each other. The object of the game is to score the most points by factoring numbers correctly. Points are scored only when every team member answers correctly.

3. Toss a coin to determine which team goes first. Hand the first student in the row the ball and say a number aloud. The student replies with any two factors of that number; record the factors on the chalkboard. For example, if you give the first student the number 56, the student might say "7 times 8." If correct, the student passes the ball to the next student on the team.

4. Give another number to the student now holding the ball. As long as the students in the first team answer questions correctly, continue down their line. If the last student on the team factors his or her number correctly, the team gets 2 points. Then the ball passes to the other team.

5. If a team member factors a number incorrectly, the ball goes to the opposing team. Begin with the first student in that line. If the opposing team member answers correctly, continue tossing out numbers to the remaining team members of that team until you reach the end of the line or until an incorrect answer is given.

6. Each time the ball reaches the end of a team, award the team 2 points and start again with the other team. Play eight rounds. The team with the highest score wins.

ASSESSMENT

If students have difficulty, suggest that they think of a number by which the number you have given can be divided evenly.

Grouping

Two teams

You'll Need

◆ Classroom chairs
◆ Small ball or beanbag
◆ A list of numbers to factor

Teaching Tip

Allow students who are stumped to call a time-out to receive coaching from fellow team members. If this results in many time-outs, you can either deduct a half-point from the final score for each time-out, or decide on a specific number of time-outs for a game.

Multiplication Wild Card

Students will enjoy this fast-paced card game featuring multiplication as the wild card.

Grouping

Two teams

You'll Need

◆ Deck of playing cards

Writing Connection

Ask students to write an explanation of the strategies they used to play Multiplication Wild Card. Ask them to explain when it is advantageous to add and when is it better to multiply in this game.

DIRECTIONS

1. Ask students to form two teams. Set up two rows of seats facing each other. Leave an aisle between the rows for your to walk.

2. Shuffle the deck of cards and stand in front of the first student. Draw the top card from the deck and show it to the whole class. Then pick a second card and show it to the first student. This is the "play" card.

3. Explain that students must look at the numbers and suits of the two cards that have been drawn. Number cards are used as factors or addends at face value. Jacks represent 10, Queens, 11, and Kings 12. If the "play" card is a spade, club, or diamond, the student can choose to add or multiply the numbers. If the second card is a heart, the student MUST multiply. Hearts are the multiplication wild card!

4. Have the first student use the two cards to choose and then perform the addition or multiplication. Award 1 point to a team when a player correctly solves an addition problem. Award 3 points for correct solutions to multiplication problems. A correct answer to a wild card problem earns 4 points. If an answer is incorrect, the next player on the opposing team takes over.

5. Play until all players on each team have had at least one turn to respond. Ask students to discuss their reasons for choosing to add or multiply when it is their turn.

ASSESSMENT

You may want to call a time-out for a discussion of a difficult problem or in cases where students disagree about an answer.

✛✛✛ VARIATION

Pairs of students can play the game. Each student would keep his or her own score, and alternate for a set amount of time. The player with more points wins the round.

Piggy Poetry

With this silly poem, students practice reading carefully for clues for using division and other math operations.

DIRECTIONS

1. This activity helps students relate dividing a quantity by 2 and finding half of the quantity. Ask the class to start with the number 84. Tell half of the class to divide 84 by 2. Tell the others to find half of 84. Allow them to use counters, draw pictures, or use any other method they like. What do they discover? Ask students from each group to explain how they got their answers.

2. Tell students they can take half or divide by 2 as they help Farmer Fred figure out how many pigs he has. Distribute reproducible page 26 and ask a volunteer to read the poem aloud. Then have students work independently to answer the questions.

3. When students are finished, have them compare answers and discuss how they figured out each one.

ASSESSMENT

Ask students to share how they figured out how many pigs the farmer had at the end of the day. **Answers: 1.** 72 pigs **2.** 72 ÷ 2 = 36 pigs each; the farmer has 36 pigs after meeting the frowning fellow **3.** 5 pigs **4.** 8 pigs; 16 pigs ÷ 2 = 8 pigs each **5.** 8

VARIATION

Students can use counters to simulate the action of the poem, starting with 72 counters for the 72 pigs.

Grouping

Individual

You'll Need

For each student:

◆ Piggy Poetry (reproducible page 26)

◆ Pencil

Teaching Tip

It might be helpful for students to underline important clues as they read the poem.

Writing Connection

On the back of the reproducible, students might enjoy writing a sequel to the poem that tells what happens to the money the farmer earned from selling his pigs.

Piggy Poetry

Read the poem. How many pigs does Farmer Fred have at the end of the day?

Pigs

Oh kind friend, hear my story
I had 72 pigs in my old black lorry.
On my journey into town
I met a fellow wearing a frown.
He said, "If I dance a jolly jig,
will you give me half your pigs?"
He danced and danced and danced so fine
I gave him half my pigs in no time!

Now away, away down the road went he,
When a lady stopped and begged for 20.
And because she had 4 lovely daughters,
I split the 20 into quarters.

Then a gentleman with a pie
happened next to wander by.
He said, "Here's what we will do:
We'll split the rest of your pigs in two.
Half for you and half for me.
Won't that surely a bargain be?"
I said yes and we ate some pie.
He took his pigs and said good-bye.

When I finally arrived at the market then,
How many pigs were in left in my pen?

1. How many pigs did Farmer Fred start with? _____

2. Write a math problem that describes what happened when Farmer Fred met the frowning

fellow. _____

How many pigs did he have when the fellow left? _____

3. How many pigs did each of the lady's daughters get? _____

4. How many pigs did the pie man get? _____

How do you know? _____

5. How many pigs did Farmer Fred end up taking to the market? _____

50+ Super-Fun Math Activities: Grade 5 © 2010 by Scholastic Inc.

Divide-O!

This division game sharpens students' understanding of division with remainders.

DIRECTIONS

1. Tell students they will be playing a division game. Explain that you'll give them some counters, and the object of the game is to divide the counters evenly without any remainders.

2. Divide the class into small groups. Distribute 50 counters to each group and then announce a number, for example, 6. This is the divisor all teams must use. All groups try to divide their 50 counters into 6 equal parts. *(They'll end up with 6 groups of 8 counters each, and a remainder of 2.)*

3. Pick a team and have them pass their "remainder pieces" to the team to their left. Ask that team: Can you make another whole set of 8 pieces? *(no)* Have them pass the collective pile of remainders to the team on their left. Continue until a team can divide their counters evenly. That team yells, "Divide-O!"

4. Now give a new number for a divisor and have teams divide with the counters they have remaining. The team that yelled Divide-O last time is the first to pass their remainders away—if they have any. Move in a clockwise direction around the room.

5. Play for a set amount of time. Award 1 point to each team that yells Divide-O. The team with the most points at the end of the time allotted wins.

 **ASSESSMENT**

Ask students to explain what they learned about division and remainders from playing the game.

 **VARIATION**

Play the game with a different number of counters to start.

Grouping
Small groups

You'll Need
◆ 50 counters for each group

Divisibility Rules!

Using the rules for dividing by 3, 4, and 5, students sort out the real kings and queens in this party of impostors!

Grouping

Individual

You'll Need

For each student:

- **Divisibility Rules! (reproducible page 29)**
- Pencil

DIRECTIONS

1. Tell the following story to students:

   Once upon a time, the King of Divisor and the Queen of Divvy-Up held a masquerade party. People from both kingdoms came. The problem was, everyone came dressed as kings and queens. Who were the Divisors? Who were the Divvy-Uppers? And who were the real King and Queen? You can figure it out with the clues on the Divisibility Rules! reproducible.

2. Distribute reproducible page 29 and review the directions with the class. Have them identify the Divisors and Divvy-Uppers, and the King and Queen.

3. When everyone has finished the activity, discuss students' findings. Make lists on the chalkboard of numbers divisible by 3 and those divisible by 4. See if students can find commonalities in the numbers in each list to generate these divisibility rules:

   - A number is divisible by 3 if the sum of its digits can be divided by 3. For example, 354 is divisible by 3 because 3 + 5 + 4 = 12, which is divisible by 3.
   - A number is divisible by 4 if the last two digits of the number can be divided by 4. For example, 724 is divisible by 4 because 24 is divisible by 4.
   - A number is divisible by 5 if the number ends in 5 or 0.

ASSESSMENT

For students having difficulty, write out the division rules and ask them to find some numbers that follow each rule. **Answers:** Numbers divisible by 3 (Divisors): 141, 294, 762, 138, and 2,622. Numbers divisible by 4 (Divvy-Uppers): 92; 1,016; 932; 9,244; and 3,452. The real King is 370; the real Queen is 125.

EXTENSION

Duplicate the masquerade with your class. Make flash cards of numbers divisible by 3, 4, and 5. (Include only two numbers divisible by 5.) Have students randomly select one card and identify themselves as Divisors or Divvy-Uppers. Who are the King and Queen?

Divisibility Rules!

Here's how to figure out who's who.

◆ Anyone wearing a number divisible by 3 is a Divisor.
Circle their numbers.

◆ Anyone wearing a number divisible by 4 is a Divvy-Upper.
Put an X through their numbers.

◆ Who are the real King and Queen? They're wearing number
divisible by 5. Put a square around their numbers.

The Troll and the Pies

Students will enjoy this delightful geometry story about a not-so-cunning troll and a clever pie lady.

Grouping

Small groups

You'll Need

For each group:

◆ **The Troll and the Pies (reproducible page 31)**

◆ 36 counters

◆ Paper

◆ Pencils

Writing Connection

Ask students to write their own stories exploring square numbers. They can tell more about the adventures of the foolish troll—or create entirely new characters.

DIRECTIONS

1. Explain to students that they'll be reading a story about a tricky troll and a clever pie lady. They will use their counters to act out the story.

2. Distribute reproducible page 31. You might have a student read aloud and pause at each place where it's time for work with counters, or allow the groups to complete the reproducible on their own.

3. When students are finished with the story, ask them to use their "pies" to make as many of their own pie triangles as possible. If a number cannot be made into a triangle, students should try to make a square. Have them list all their triangle numbers and all their square numbers.

4. Ask students which numbers formed triangles and which formed squares. Then ask students if they can find a number that is both triangular and square.

ASSESSMENT

Answers: Triangular numbers that can be formed with 36 counters are 3, 6, 10, 16, 21, and 28. Square numbers are 4, 9, 15, and 25. The number 36 is both square and triangular.

Name _____

The Troll and the Pies

Read the story.
Act it out with counters.

In a house in the wood lived a pie lady. All day long she baked pies. One night, before she went to sleep, she placed her pies in her window like this:

Set up your counters like the pies.
When you're done, keep reading.

That night, a troll swallowed one of the pies. He laughed to himself, "What a fool the pie lady is, to leave her pies out like this!" Then he saw that the pies looked like this:

Change your "pies" to look like this.
When you're done, keep reading.

"If I leave them like this," said the troll, "the pie lady will know someone has gobbled a pie. I know—I will move the pies around to make another triangle!" But try as he might, the troll couldn't turn the 14 pies into a triangle. Worried, he gobbled up 4 more pies, and was left with this:

Change your "pies" to look like this.
Then keep reading.

"It's a triangle!" he thought. "But it is too small! She'll know that 5 are missing." He thought some more, and ate another pie. He moved them around and was left with this:

Change your "pies" to look like this.
Then keep reading.

"Oh no!" he cried. "That's a square, not a triangle! Oh, what a fix I am in!"

The troll was so upset that he ate up all the remaining pies and dashed off into the woods. All night long he had quite a bellyache. In the morning the wise pie lady found him. "You silly troll," said the pie lady. "You were too, too greedy! And you don't know math, either!"

31

Grouping

Individual

You'll Need

For each student:

◆ **Where Did Hy Hide My Pie? (reproducible page 33)**

◆ Metric ruler

◆ Pencils

Teaching Tip

If you don't have enough rulers, students can mark off the map scale with a pencil along the edge of an index card.

Where Did Hy Hide My Pie?

Students use compass directions to find out where Hyman, the baker, hid a customer's gooseberry pie.

DIRECTIONS

1. Tell this story to students:

   The baker Hyman Crisp thinks it's funny to hide his customers' pies. When people pay for their pies, Hyman gives them a piece of paper with compass directions on it. If the customers follow the directions correctly, they'll find their pies.

2. Distribute reproducible page 33 and tell students that the picture they see shows the situation facing Hy's latest customer. The scale on the map explains that 1 centimeter stands for 10 meters. You might explain to students how to read the directions:

   40 meters SW

   This tells you how many meters to walk.

   This tells you in which direction to walk.

   So 40 meters SW would measure 4 cm southwest on the map.

3. Ask students to use the compass directions to find the pie. They can measure and draw lines on the map to show the correct route.

ASSESSMENT

The pie is hidden under the manhole cover on the far right of the map. Students should have drawn a zigzag line leading from Hy's Pies to the pie.

▶▶▶ EXTENSION

For a real challenge, ask students to write the directions from the manhole back to Hy's shop. It's tough! The distances will remain the same, but they'll have to reverse the compass directions.

50+ Super-Fun Math Activities: Grade 5 © 2010 by Scholastic Inc.

Name _____

Where Did Hy Hide My Pie?

Help the Hyman Crisp's customer find his gooseberry pie. Follow the directions and you'll find the pie. When you find the spot, mark it with a big X.

DIRECTIONS

60 meters NE
20 meters E
50 meters SW
80 meters SE
40 meters NE
40 meters NW
40 meters NE
90 meters SE

BURGER PALACE

HY'S PIES

Scale: 1 cm = 10m

0   10   20   30   40   50 meters

N   NE   E   SE   S   SW   W   NW

33

Get the Scoop on Cereal

In this activity, students become savvy consumers when they see how much cereal they're getting for their money.

Grouping

Small groups

You'll Need

For each group:
◆ Empty cereal box

Writing Connection

Have students write an evaluative article, similar to one found in *Consumer Reports*, discussing what they have discovered about the cereals they surveyed. Ask them to use graphs or illustrations to clarify their points.

PREPARATION

Ask volunteers to bring in an empty cereal box, or purchase a box of cereal for each group. Be sure you have a record of the price of each box.

DIRECTIONS

1. Ask students to tell you their favorite cereal. Explain to students that they will be conducting an experiment to see what they're getting for their money when they buy cereal. Distribute a box of cereal to each group and ask students to record the weight as printed on the box. Then have students find the price and calculate the unit price of the cereal. *(Formula: price of box ÷ number of ounces = unit price, or price per ounce.)*

2. Tell students that another way to look at the value they're getting for their money is to find the price per serving of their cereal. Have students find the number of servings per container in the nutritional information on the side of the box. Ask students to calculate the cereal's serving price, that is, how much they're paying for one serving of cereal. *(Formula: price of box ÷ number of servings = serving price.)*

3. Discuss students' results and compile the results in a chart by type of cereal. How does the unit price compare to price per serving for each cereal? Which cereal is the best buy?

ASSESSMENT

Ask students what features determine a "better" buy. Is price the only factor? What else determines whether a cereal is a better buy?

➜➜➜ EXTENSION

Have students calculate unit price and serving price for their favorite brand of cereal at home.

A Wheely Good Time!

*Students use a handmade measuring wheel
to measure some distances in and around school.*

PREPARATION
You may want to make the measuring wheels ahead of time. If
students will make their own, set up a work station for each group.

DIRECTIONS
1. Divide the class into groups and explain that they will make a
   simple measuring wheel—a tool used by engineers, police officers,
   and architects to measure distances. To make a measuring wheel:

   ◆ Punch a hole through the center of the plastic coffee can lid.
     Attach the lid to the ruler with the brass fastener.

   ◆ Stick masking tape around the circumference of the lid. This will
     provide some friction if the wheel is used on a slick surface.

   ◆ Make a mark on the circumference
     of the lid. Wrap a piece of string
     around the circumference, mark the
     string where it meets, and measure
     its length. Round this number to
     the nearest half inch or inch, and
     write the number on the lid.

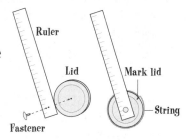

2. When their wheels are made, have students pick a distance in
   the classroom or school and work in their groups to estimate that
   distance. Then have one student roll the wheel while other group
   members keep track of the number of times the wheel goes
   around, using the mark on the lid.

3. To calculate the distance, students multiply the number of inches
   on the wheel by the number of times the wheel went around.
   With a large number of inches, students can convert the inches
   to feet (divide by 12) or yards (divide by 36).

✦✦✦ VARIATION
Have one group use the measuring wheel to find a given distance
while another group uses a ruler or yardstick to measure the same
distance. Which was easier? Which was more accurate? Why?

➡➡➡ EXTENSION
Allow students to borrow the measuring wheels to measure some
distances at home.

Grouping
Small groups

You'll Need

◆ Rulers with a hole at
  one end, one for
  each wheel

◆ Plastic coffee can
  lids, one for each
  wheel

◆ Brass fasteners

◆ String

◆ Marker

◆ Masking tape

Writing Connection

Have students take
some measurements in
the classroom or on the
play area and then
write directions from
one spot to a "mystery
spot," using numbers
of wheels in their
directions. For example:
Start at the slide. Go
north 15 wheels. Go
east 12 wheels. Where
are you?

Tooling for Measurement

As they move around the game board, students decide which measuring tool is best for a certain measuring task.

DIRECTIONS

1. Ask students what tool they would use to measure length, temperature, weight, volume, and time. For most of these situations, students should be able to name several appropriate tools.

2. Explain that students will use what they know about measurement tools as they play a game. The object of the game is to go from START to END and receive the most points.

3. Assign pairs and distribute reproducible page 37, playing pieces, and a paper clip to each pair. Show students how to spin a paper clip around the point of a pencil placed at the center of the spinner. Students spin, and the highest number goes first. The first player spins and moves ahead that number of spaces. The student looks at the picture he or she landed on and names a measuring tool that could be used to measure the object or action.

4. After the first player announces the measuring tool, the opponent must consider whether to accept it. If the tool is approved, 2 points are awarded. If not, the first player is allowed a chance to explain. If the selection is still contested, no points are awarded. (The teacher may be called in to referee if needed.) Play continues until both players reach or pass the END. The player with more points wins.

5. After the game is played, ask students to discuss the most hotly-debated objects or actions. Ask them if there is only one way to measure something—or does it depend on the information they are looking for.

Grouping

Pairs

You'll Need

For each pair:

◆ **Tooling for Measurement (reproducible page 37)**

◆ 2 counters (playing pieces)

◆ Paper

◆ Pencils

◆ Paper clip

ASSESSMENT

Most objects on the board can be interpreted in more than one way. Check to see how each pair is dealing with this challenge.

➔➔➔ EXTENSION

Have each student find pictures of two or three objects and paste or tape them to a sheet of paper. Next to each one, students should list as many measurement tools as they can that might be used to measure the object.

Name _____

Tooling for Measurement

PICK YOUR TOOL!

Tape measure · Thermometer · Scale · clock

Cup · Yardstick · Ruler · Protractor

SKIP TURN · 1 · 2 · SKIP TURN · 3 · 4

START · SHOE · SNOW · PAINT · THERMOMETER BREAKS LOSE 1 TURN

COLLAR · BALLOON

RULER SNAPS! GO BACK 2 · WORM · CANDY · SUN

CAR WHEEL · MILK · GATOR · BREAD · WAKE UP · CHEESE · HAND · RICE

BLACK HOLE LOSE 2 TURNS

END · GOLDFISH · PENNY · TRAIN

Problems and More

Put on your thinking cap to solve these problems.

1. SAILING AWAY!

In ancient Constantinople, sailmakers made eight sails a day, seven days a week. If each boat needs three sails, how many three-sail ships can sail from Constantinople at the end of one week?

_____

Look it up! Today Constantinople is known as Istanbul, Turkey. Can you find it on a map of the world?

2. OUR PAL, THE PALINDROME

What's a palindrome? It's a number like 1001 or 23432 that reads the same way backward as forward. The thing about palindromes is that you never know where they'll pop up. What if a car odometer (the device that shows the car's mileage) reads 12021? How many miles must pass before the next palindrome?

_____

What will that palindrome be?

_____

3. MAGIC CALCULATIONS

Try this problem as many times as you like. No matter what you do, your answer will always be 1,089!

EXAMPLE:

Step 1	583
Step 2	−385
Step 3	198
Step 4	+891
Step 5	1,089

Step 1: Chose a number made up of 3 different digits. The difference between the first and third digits must be at least 2.

Step 2: Write your number backward.

Step 3: Subtract the smaller number from the larger one.

Step 4: Write the answer to Step 3 backward.

Step 5: Add the answers to Steps 3 and 4.

4. FINDING FIBONACCI'S PATTERN

Leonardo Fibonacci lived in Italy during the Middle Ages. He was the greatest mathematician of his day. His fame rests on a series of numbers he found called the Fibonacci Sequence. Here's how it starts. Can you figure out the next five numbers?

1, 1, 2, 3, 5, 8, 13, 21, 34,

___ , ___ , ___ , ___ , ___ .

50+ Super-Fun Math Activities: Grade 5 © 2010 by Scholastic Inc.

Answers on page 64.

Problems and More

5. PIGS IN A PEN

Put each of these pigs in its own pen by drawing only three straight lines.

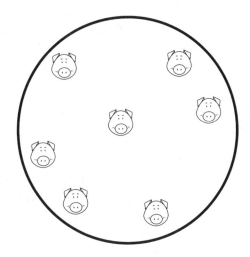

6. ANCHORS A-WEIGH!

Three animals want to cross a lake in a boat. There's an ape that weighs 800 pounds, a bear that weighs 500 pounds, and a lion that weighs 300 pounds. Their boat can hold only 800 pounds. They can't swim across the lake, walk around it, or hang off the edge of the boat.

How can they use the boat to get across the lake? Can you tell who is in the boat for each trip? (Hint: The animals make five crossings.)

7. AROUND WE GO!

Using only the numbers 4 through 12, fill in the circles so that the numbers on each straight line add up to 21.

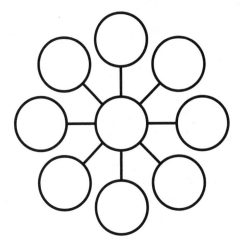

8. A WHALE OF A PROBLEM

The blue whale is the largest animal on earth. It weighs 297,000 pounds. Compared to the blue whale, an elephant is puny! It weighs only 16,500 pounds! What if you wanted to balance this scale. How many elephants would you have to put in the empty pan?

50+ Super-Fun Math Activities: Grade 5 © 2010 by Scholastic Inc.

Grouping

Small groups

You'll Need

For each group:

◆ **Dis-Count of Monte Cristo (reproducible page 41)**

◆ Counters (game pieces)

◆ Paper clip

◆ Paper

◆ Pencils

The Dis-Count of Monte Cristo

Everything in the Count's gift shop is on sale, and fractions can help students figure out how much they save!

DIRECTIONS

1. Are students savvy shoppers? Tell them they'll be playing a discount shopping game, competing against other teams. The object of the game is to stroll through the Count's gift shop—but to reach the end having saved the most money!

2. Distribute reproducible page 41. Point out to students that they are working with a double spinner. Each player spins twice in each turn. Show students how spin a paper clip around the point of a pencil placed at the center of the spinner.

3. On the first spin, students move their game piece ahead the number of spaces shown on the inner spinner. They record the item and its price. Then they spin again. The second spin tells them what fraction of the original price they can deduct. Team members work to decide if they can subtract that fraction of the price from their purchase. For example, if they land on a $16 pair of golf shoes, and spin ½ off, they can solve this problem to calculate the savings of $8.

4. Some problems cannot be solved evenly. For example, ⅓ of $16 results in a mixed number, 5⅓, or about $5.33. When this happens, the team loses a turn. They can move ahead only when their fractions-off calculation results in an amount ending in either 5 or 0 ($15, $15.25, $15.50, $15.30, etc.).

5. Since this is a team effort, each student on a team must agree that they've done the math correctly before each turn ends. The game continues until all players on a team have passed the finish line. Then teams compare savings, and the group with the highest dollar amount in savings wins.

→→→ EXTENSIONS

◆ Have the class look for fraction-off prices in a local newspaper. Have them find the sale prices and figure out how much could be saved on each purchase.

◆ When students are working with percent, they can play the game again. Use correction fluid on a copy of the reproducible to change the spinner from fractions to percents.

The Dis-Count of Monte Cristo

A Dollar for Your Fraction

To gain an understanding of the fractional parts of a dollar, students fold and cut fractions.

DIRECTIONS

1. Explain to students that they are going to show fractional parts of one dollar. Remind students that a dollar represents 100 cents. Each penny is $\frac{1}{100}$ of a dollar. An equation expressing this would be $\frac{1}{100} + \frac{1}{100} + \frac{1}{100}$ and so on, one hundred times. Cutting a dollar bill into 100 equal pieces would be another way to show this.

2. Distribute copies of the dollar to each group and ask students to fold and cut each one into a different number of fractional pieces. Tell them that at least one of their fractions should be equivalent to an actual coin. For example, what fractional part of a dollar is a quarter? a dime? a nickel? a penny? Ask students to paste their fraction pieces for each dollar to make a "picture equation" that shows how a dollar can be expressed with it. For example, a dollar may be cut into four equal pieces and then pasted and labeled as follows:

$$\frac{1}{4} + \frac{1}{4} + \frac{1}{4} + \frac{1}{4} = \$1$$

ASSESSMENT

Ask students how many different combinations of fractions they can make that have actual coin representations. *(5: 2 half-dollars, 4 quarters, 10 dimes, 20 nickels, 100 pennies)*

✦✦✦ VARIATION

Make the problems more challenging by asking students to write a fraction equation using fractions that represent two different U.S. coins. Ask them to check that their equation works. (They'll need to find a least common denominator, since their denominators will all be different: $\frac{1}{100}$, $\frac{1}{5}$, $\frac{1}{10}$, $\frac{1}{25}$ or even $\frac{1}{50}$.)

You'll Need

For each group:
- ◆ Play dollar bill photocopy
- ◆ Paper
- ◆ Pencils
- ◆ Scissors
- ◆ Glue or tape

Dog-Gone Decimals!

Students help the dogcatcher round up some runaways as they add and subtract decimals.

DIRECTIONS

1. Review how to add and subtract decimals. Be sure students recall these important points: They must always align the decimal points, and they can add any number of zeros at the end of a decimal number to create workable numbers for a subtraction example.

2. Distribute reproducible page 44 and tell students they are going to help the dogcatcher round up some strays. The object is to be the first to round up three strays.

3. Show students how to use the spinner, by spinning a paper clip around the point of a pencil placed at the center of the spinner. Players spin; the player with the higher number goes first. When it is a player's turn, he or she spins and moves ahead that number of spaces.

4. If a player lands on a decimal number, that number is added to the player's score. If players land on a dog space, they must subtract that number from their score. If a player lands on the Dogcatcher's Office space on an exact spin, that player adds .75 to his or her score.

   The player who reaches (or passes) the Dogcatcher's office with the higher score wins the round and has "caught" one dog. Play continues for additional rounds until a player catches three dogs to win the game.

 ASSESSMENT

Observe students as they play the game. Be sure they are regrouping to subtract from zero when necessary.

VARIATION

You can make the game more difficult by adding a whole number before each of the decimal numbers on the game board.

 **Grouping**

Pairs

You'll Need

For each pair:

◆ **Dog-Gone Decimals! (reproducible page 44)**

◆ 2 counters (game pieces)

◆ Paper

◆ Pencils

◆ Paper clips

 **Writing Connection**

Ask students to write a brief paragraph in which they tell which series of decimals they'd rather land on to win this game and why. .4111, .127, OR .2, .3, .003.

Dog-Gone Decimals!

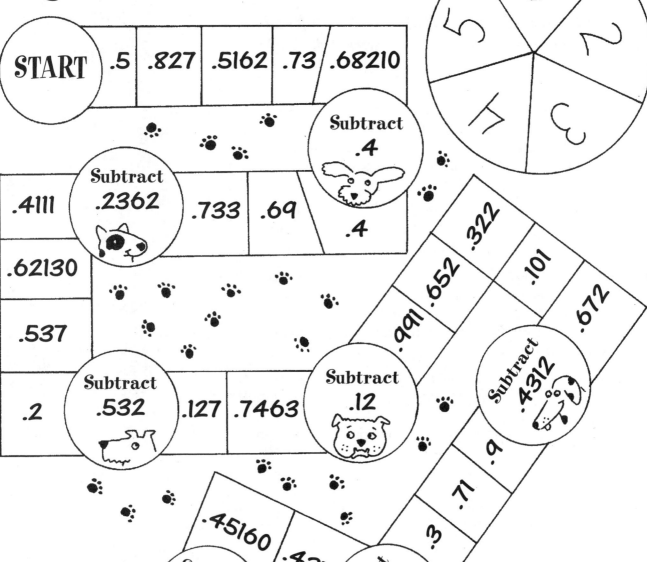

START | .5 | .827 | .5162 | .73 | .68210

Spinner: 1 2 3 4 5

.4111 | Subtract .2362 | .733 | .69 | Subtract .4 | .4

.62130 | .537 | .2 | Subtract .532 | .127 | .7463

Subtract .12 | .991 | .652 | .322 | .101 | .672 | Subtract .4312

.9 | .71 | .3 | Subtract .532 | .45160 | .437

Subtract .2362 | .003 | .3 | .71717

Subtract .4312 | .5001 | .2601 | Subtract .12 | Subtract .4

DOGCATCHER'S OFFICE

50+ Super-Fun Math Activities: Grade 5 © 2010 by Scholastic Inc.

Let's Make 1!

Students get practice working with decimals as they play this decimal version of tic-tack-toe.

DIRECTIONS

1. What are some decimals that can be added to make 1? Review adding decimals, such as .61 and .39. What is the sum? Ask volunteers to give you other examples of decimals whose sum is 1.

2. Distribute reproducible page 46 and explain the object of the game: to shade any squares on the decimal board to add up to a sum of 1. Students can take turns going first. The starting player shades as many squares as he or she needs to make 1. Example: SHADE .32 + .45 + .22 + .01 = 1.

3. As the game progresses, students take turns coloring in squares that make 1. Each student uses his or her own color. If a box has been shaded, it cannot be used again. The game is over when the number 1 cannot be made with any of the remaining numbers on the board. The winner is the student who made 1 more times.

4. Ask students to discuss their strategies for winning the game. If they didn't win, what would they do differently next time?

ASSESSMENT

Observe students as they play. Do they pick numbers randomly, or do they use the organizational pattern of the number board to devise strategies for quickly finding decimals that add up to 1?

✦✦✦ VARIATION

Place restrictions on the play of the game. For example, students can make 1 by shading two boxes only, or three boxes only, and so on.

Grouping

Pairs

You'll Need

For each pair:

◆ **Let's Make 1! (reproducible page 46)**

◆ 2 different-color crayons

◆ Paper

◆ Pencils

Let's Make 1!

.01	.02	.03	.04	.05	.06	.07	.08	.09	.10
.11	.12	.13	.14	.15	.16	.17	.18	.19	.20
.21	.22	.23	.24	.25	.26	.27	.28	.29	.30
.31	.32	.33	.34	.35	.36	.37	.38	.39	.40
.41	.42	.43	.44	.45	.46	.47	.48	.49	.50
.51	.52	.53	.54	.55	.56	.57	.58	.59	.60
.61	.62	.63	.64	.65	.66	.67	.68	.69	.70
.71	.72	.73	.74	.75	.76	.77	.78	.79	.80
.81	.82	.83	.84	.85	.86	.87	.88	.89	.90
.91	.92	.93	.94	.95	.96	.97	.98	.99	

50+ Super-Fun Math Activities: Grade 5 © 2010 by Scholastic Inc.

Decimal-Fraction Olympics

Students use fractions and decimals to describe their proficiency in simple classroom athletics.

PREPARATION

Clear a space in the classroom large enough to allow student to toss a beanbag or foam ball into an empty trash can from about 12 feet away. Use masking tape to mark a line on the floor where students are to stand.

DIRECTIONS

1. Explain to students that they will be shooting baskets and recording their tries to write fractions and decimals. Appoint a scorekeeper. Ask each team to step up to the mark on the floor and take turns trying to shoot baskets. Have each student make two sets of five shot: Trial 1 and Trial 2. Ask students to name a fraction that shows the successful number of shots out of the given number of attempts.

2. Ask students to analyze their data. What fraction of the shots did each player make? What fraction of the shots did the team make? What fraction did the whole class make? You may wish to review certain concepts, such as how to use the data to generate a fraction. Each fraction might be expressed this way:

   Number of successful shots
   ———————————————
   Number of attempted shots

   To convert their fractions to decimals, remind students they can divide the numerator by the denominator.

 **EXTENSION**

Challenge students to convert their fraction or decimal numbers into decimals, and then percentages. Their goal might be to answer this question: What percentage of your shots did you make?

 **Grouping**
Small groups

 **You'll Need**

◆ Paper
◆ Pencils
◆ Soft beanbag or foam ball
◆ Trash can

 Teaching Tip

If you have more balls and trash cans, you can set up several shooting stations.

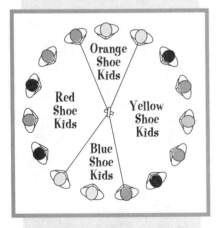

Shoo, Graph, Shoe!

In this whole-class activity, students get a visual picture of the meaning of circle graphs and how to interpret them.

PREPARATION

On the chalkboard, write the following colors: red, blue, green, orange, yellow, purple.

DIRECTIONS

1. Invite the class to make a graph of shoe colors. Distribute the drawing paper and crayons. Ask students to select one color from the list on the chalkboard and use it to draw and color a shoe. They can be as creative as they like in designing the type of shoe, as long as they use only that one color.

2. When drawings are completed, students should find others in the class who used the same color for their shoes. Ask groups with each color to gather in one spot.

3. Now have students come together in their groups to form a large circle. Each group should stay together within the circle, so all the green shoes are together, all the blues are together, and so on. Have students sit down in a circle and place their "shoe sheets" in front of them.

4. Hand a piece of string or yarn to the first "blue shoe" and bring one end of that piece into the middle of the circle. Tape it down in the center. Do this for the last "blue shoe" also. Repeat with each shoe color.

5. After each color is "linked" by string, discuss the representation. Ask questions such as these:

   ◆ How many shoes are in the circle?

   ◆ Can you think of a fraction (percent) that describes the whole circle?

   ◆ Can you think of a fraction (percent) that describes the number of red shoes in the circle? blue shoes?

   ◆ Of all the orange and yellow shoes, what fraction (percent) are yellow?

⇥⇥⇥ EXTENSION

Ask students to find examples of circle graphs and post them on a bulletin board. They can use fractions or percents to label shaded parts to show the approximate part of the circle each section represents.

Birthday Scatter Plot

Students use a scatter plot to draw conclusions about their birthdays.

PREPARATION

Before class, draw a pair of horizontal and vertical axes on the chalkboard and label the vertical axis from top to bottom with the months of the year. Label the horizontal axis with the numbers 1 through 31.

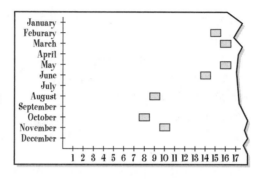

Grouping

Whole class

You'll Need

◆ Stick-on notes, one for each student

DIRECTIONS

1. Explain to students that they will use a scatter plot to show information about their birthdays. Distribute stick-on notes to students. Invite them to come to the chalkboard and place the note on the graph on their birthday month and date.

2. Explain to students that they've just made a scatter plot. Information can be obtained from the graph based on how the notes are scattered across it.

3. Ask students questions about the scatter plot such as: In what month were the majority of students in the class born? How do you know? On what date or dates were the most people born?

ASSESSMENT

Ask students to name instances in which a scatter plot graph would be the best way to record information.

▶▶▶ EXTENSIONS

◆ Ask students to imagine what a birthday scatter plot for everyone in the school would look like. Ask students questions such as: How would the graph be different? How might it be similar? Do you think the same days and months would have the most birthdays? Why or why not?

◆ Ask students to look at the information on the scatter plot and determine if there is another type of graph that could represent the information accurately.

Writing Connection

Ask students to design their own scatter plot graphs. Have them write a paragraph that describes the axes and tells about the kind of information they hope to obtain.

Grouping

Whole class

You'll Need

◆ Clothespins, one for each student and yourself

◆ Ribbon or heavy rope

◆ Index cards or small pieces of paper

It's a Mean Average!

Students gather data and represent averages—both median and mean.

PREPARATION

Before class, tack 12-inch lengths of ribbon or rope to a bulletin board. Post a number above each piece, from 1 to 8.

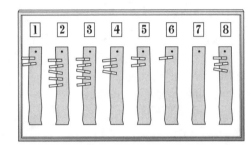

DIRECTIONS

1. Tell students they're going to take a sibling survey. You might begin by telling them how many siblings there are in your own family. Show students how to record that information by clipping a clothespin on the ribbon under the appropriate number.

2. Give each student a clothespin. Have students come up, one at a time, and clip their clothespins to show the number of siblings in their family. If a student is an only child, she or he would clip 1. If there are 2 children in the family, clip 2, and so on.

3. When all students have recorded their data, use them to discuss averages. Ask students what the middle number is. For example, if the number of siblings in the class range from 0 to 8, the middle number is 4. That number is the *median*. Then show students how to create an approximate *mean*, or average, by moving clothespins until the number on each ribbon is as equal as it can be. By "evening off" the data, students are approximating an average.

4. If you want, show students how to calculate the average by adding the numbers and then dividing the sum by the number of addends. How close is that number to the average students found by moving clothespins?

 ASSESSMENT
Observe to see if students can record and interpret the data.

➔➔➔ EXTENSION
Leave the clothespin graph displayed and ask students to use the data to create a pictograph or bar graph. Have them show their graphs and ask the rest of the class to evaluate whether the data are shown accurately.

My Lucky Number

Students collect data as they investigate why some numbers come up more frequently than others in games.

DIRECTIONS

1. Divide the class into small groups and distribute reproducible page 52 and number cubes. Ask students to predict which sums will come up most often when two number cubes are rolled. After sharing some ideas, set students rolling! Ask them to roll the two cubes twenty times. Each time they roll, they record their results, paying attention to which number comes up on each cube. Ask them to record both numbers on the tally sheet. For example, if they roll a 4 and a 3, they record the roll above the number 7 on their tally sheet as a sum like this: 4 + 3.

Their goal is to see how many different ways they can make numbers between 2 and 12. So if they roll a 5 and a 2, they write this sum on the their tally sheet in the same column for 7 above the earlier sum of 4 + 3.

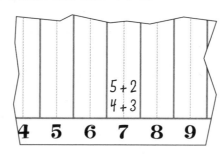

2. If students roll a combination they've already recorded on the tally sheet, they do not record it again. However, students should count opposite rolls of the dice, such as 5 + 2 and 2 + 5, as two separate combinations.

3. If students have completed their twentieth roll and there are still some open spaces on the chart, have them roll another twenty times.

4. Discuss students' findings. Ask them to evaluate their predictions: Did the sums they predicted would come up most often actually do this? Ask questions to help students evaluate their data. For example: Which columns took longest to fill? Which numbers have the most combinations? Which have the least? Why do you think this is so?

ASSESSMENT

From the activity they've just done, ask students if they think any number can be considered "lucky." Why do they think so? *(There are 6 possible combinations for the number 7, more than any other; and 5 ways to make 6 and 8.)*

Grouping
Small groups

You'll Need

For each group:

◆ **My Lucky Number (reproducible page 52)**

◆ Two 1–6 number cubes of different colors

◆ Paper

◆ Pencils

Names _____

52

My Lucky Number

2	3	4	5	6	7	8	9	10	11	12

Math Mystery Bags

Students use probability to determine how many candies, and which kinds, are contained in three mystery bags.

PREPARATION

For each group, set up the candies in the three bags in these proportions: Bag 1: 20 type A, 5 type B; Bag 2: 15 type A, 10 type B; and Bag 3: 5 type A and 20 type B. Label the bags Bag 1, Bag 2, Bag 3. On the chalkboard, write the numbers of candies you've put in the three bags—but don't say which bag is which.

DIRECTIONS

1. Show students a sample of each kind of candy and explain how you've filled the bags. Explain to students that they will be conducting an experiment to test the likelihood—the probability—of picking one kind of candy or the other from each of the three bags. Ask students to look at the numbers of candy in the bags and predict: From which bag will they get more picks of candy type A? From which should they get more picks of candy type B?

2. Divide the class into small groups and give each group reproducible page 54. Ask a student in each group to "sample" the bags: reach in without looking and take out one piece of candy. Have them mark their charts with an X corresponding to the type of candy they picked.

3. Next, tell students to replace the candy and choose another. Students can take turns and repeat the candy pick 20 times for each bag, tallying every selection on the chart.

4. When students have finished, ask them to use the data they collected to answer the questions. Then talk about their discoveries. Did their original predictions turn out to be accurate?

ASSESSMENT

Ask students to make some generalizations about the probability of choosing a specific type of candy based on how many of each type is in the bag.

▶▶▶ EXTENSION

Students can make their own mixes of type A and type B candies, keeping the same total number of candies in each bag. When they exchange bags with a classmate, can the classmate predict the number of candies of each type that are in the bags?

Grouping

Small groups

You'll Need

◆ **Math Mystery Bags (reproducible page 54),** one for each student

◆ Two different types of wrapped candies

◆ Three small paper bags for each group

Math Mystery Bags

Draw candies from the bags. Use Xs to mark the
type of candy you pull out and put back each time.

Draw	Candy _____	Candy _____
1		
2		
3		
4		
5		
6		
7		
8		
9		
10		
11		
12		
13		
14		
15		
16		
17		
18		
19		
20		

How many of each
candy do you think
is in this bag?

_____

Draw	Candy _____	Candy _____
1		
2		
3		
4		
5		
6		
7		
8		
9		
10		
11		
12		
13		
14		
15		
16		
17		
18		
19		
20		

How many of each
candy do you think
is in this bag?

_____

Draw	Candy _____	Candy _____
1		
2		
3		
4		
5		
6		
7		
8		
9		
10		
11		
12		
13		
14		
15		
16		
17		
18		
19		
20		

How many of each
candy do you think
is in this bag?

_____

50+ Super-Fun Math Activities: Grade 5 © 2010 by Scholastic Inc.

Magic Cookie Ratios

Your student put ratios to work where they belong—in the kitchen!

DIRECTIONS

1. Explain to students that cooks use ratios to increase or decrease recipes. That way, they can make more or less food than the recipe normally yields. Ratios help them increase or decrease all of the ingredients proportionally. Tell students that they will become the cooks and use ratios to increase a recipe.

2. Show students that to make lemonade, the ratio is 3 parts water to 1 part lemonade mix. Other ways to write that ratio include: 3 to 1, 3:1, and ¾₁. Draw these examples on the chalkboard:

1 cup	1 cup	1 cup	1 cup
water	water	water	lemonade mix

3. Ask students to figure out how much water would be needed if someone used 8 cups of lemonade mix. Set up the following proportion on the chalkboard:

$$\frac{3 \text{ parts water}}{1 \text{ part mix}} = \frac{?}{8 \text{ cups mix}}$$

Students can solve this proportion by cross-multiplying:

$$? \times 1 = 3 \times 8$$
$$? = 24$$

They can also solve it using manipulatives:

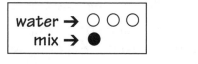

4. Distribute reproducible page 56 and have students increase the amount of each ingredient for the Magic Cookie recipe.

Grouping
Whole class

You'll Need

◆ Magic Cookie Ratios (reproducible page 56), one for each student
◆ Optional: ingredients and cooking supplies to bake the cookies (see reproducible)

Teaching Tip

If you make the cookies, check for possible food allergies ahead of time.

Magic Cookie Ratios

Below is a recipe for Magic Cookies. The recipe makes 24 bars.

1. The recipe calls for 2 parts brown sugar, 1 part butter.

What is the ratio of sugar to butter? _____

2. Write that ratio in two other ways.   a. _____   b. _____

3. You want to increase the recipe.
You decide to use 8 cups of brown sugar.
Write a proportion to figure out how much butter to use. _____

4. Now solve your proportion. How many parts butter should you use? _____

Now increase the recipe to make 48 bars and 72 bars. (The first one is done for you.)

MAGIC COOKIE RECIPE

To make 24 bars	48 bars	72 bars
2 cups brown sugar	4 cups	6 cups
2 cups flour	☐ cups	☐ cups
1 stick butter, softened	☐ sticks	☐ sticks
1 teaspoon baking powder	☐ teaspoons	☐ teaspoons
1/2 teaspoon salt	☐ teaspoons	☐ teaspoons
1 teaspoon vanilla extract	☐ teaspoons	☐ teaspoons
1 cup milk	☐ cups	☐ cups
1 egg	☐ eggs	☐ eggs
1 cup semisweet chocolate chips	☐ cups	☐ cups

TO MAKE MAGIC COOKIES

1. Preheat oven to 350°F. Lightly grease a 13-inch by 9-inch baking pan and set it aside.

2. In bowl, mix brown sugar and flour. Mix in the butter until mixture resembles crumbs. Remove 1 cup of mixture and set aside.

3. To bowl, add baking powder and salt. Using a fork, beat in the vanilla, milk, and egg. Beat until a smooth batter forms. Pour batter into prepared baking pan.

4. Sprinkle the crumbs you put aside on top of the batter in the pan. Sprinkle on chocolate chips.

5. Using spatula, spread chips and crumbs evenly over the top of batter.

6. Bake for 35 minutes or until skewer inserted in center comes out clean.

7. Transfer to wire rack. Cool bars in pan completely before slicing.

50+ Super-Fun Math Activities: Grade 5 © 2010 by Scholastic Inc.

Me and My Math Shadow!

Students learn the technique of "shadowing"—using proportions to calculate an unknown height.

PREPARATIONS

The class will need to work outside on a sunny day.

DIRECTIONS

1. Ask students how they could measure the height of a tree, flagpole, telephone pole, or other tall object. After a few minutes of discussion, tell students there's an easy way to do this using their own height, and proportion.

2. Divide the class into pairs and ask each pair to select a tall object they want to measure, such as a tree. Have one student face the sun in the same direction as the tree. Ask the other student to use the yardstick to measure her or his partner's height and record the information. Immediately following this measurement, partners should measure the shadow of the student and record the measurement. (This should be done quickly so the sun does not change position.) Finally, students should measure the shadow cast by the tree and record the measurement.

3. Explain to students that they can use the three measurements they have been able to directly measure to set up and solve a proportion to find the unknown height of their object:

$$\frac{\text{student height}}{\text{student shadow}} = \frac{\text{object height (?)}}{\text{object shadow}}$$

4. Distribute reproducible page 58 and have students complete it using trees or other tall objects near school or home. (Each time, they must take the height and shadow length of a partner first, then the shadow length of the object.)

ASSESSMENT

Ask students how their own height and length of their shadows helps them to figure out the height of the tall object.

▶▶▶ EXTENSION

Students can repeat the activity at a different time of day. Do they get the same height for the tall object(s)?

Grouping

Pairs

You'll Need

For each pair:

◆ Me and My Math Shadow! (reproducible page 58)

◆ Yardstick

◆ Pencil

Teaching Tip

Remind students that they must take all the measurements at about the same time or the sun will move and their data will be inaccurate.

Me and My Math Shadow!

1. Measure one partner's height.

2. Stand so your shadow falls in the same direction as the shadow of the object you want to measure. Measure your shadow.

3. Measure the object's shadow.

4. Set up a proportion: $\dfrac{\text{student height}}{\text{student shadow}} = \dfrac{\text{object height (?)}}{\text{object shadow}}$

Record your data on this chart.

Solve each proportion to find the object's height.

OBJECT	STUDENT'S HEIGHT	STUDENT'S SHADOW	OBJECT'S SHADOW	PROPORTION	OBJECT'S HEIGHT

Art Show Ratios

Students create their own artwork with an eye toward teaching ratios to their peers.

PREPARATION

Before class, draw a picture on the chalkboard of 3 red fish and 2 blue fish, and 6 red butterflies and 3 blue butterflies.

Grouping

Individuals

You'll Need

◆ Paper
◆ Paints
◆ Brushes
◆ Crayons
◆ Colored chalk

DIRECTIONS

1. Explain that a ratio is a way to compare two amounts. Ask students to look at the fish you drew on the chalkboard. To compare blue fish to red fish, the numbers can be expressed as a ratio in three ways: 2 to 3 or 2:3 or $\frac{2}{3}$. The order of the numbers is important. Writing 3 to 2 would give the ratio of red fish to blue fish. Ask volunteers to give these ratios:

   ◆ red butterflies to blue butterflies *(6:3)*

   ◆ fish to butterflies *(5:9)*

2. Next, tell students that you'd like them to draw their own ratio picture. They can draw animals, people, pets, or anything they want. After they've finished their drawings, ask them to write ratios that express the number of objects they have drawn.

3. When students have finished, hold a "ratio exhibit." Hang students' drawings and have the class identify some of the ratios.

ASSESSMENT

Meet with individual students to discuss their drawings and the ratios they have written. Ask students to explain their ratios.

▶▶▶ EXTENSION

Have students combine their artwork into a book with integrated text. They can donate their work to the school library.

Problems and More

Put on your thinking cap to solve these problems.

1. ODDS 'N' EVENS

Complete this puzzle using each of these numbers only once: 2, 4, 5, 7, 8, 11, 13, 14, 16.

Put the even numbers in the squares and the odd numbers in the circles.

Each row of three numbers must add up to 26.

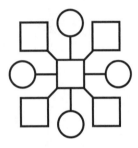

2. A HIDDEN NUMBER

Try to guess this number:
The number has three digits.
It is a multiple of 9.
Its tens digit is a factor of 16, but not a factor of 4.
Two of the number's factors are 5 and 2.

What's the number? _____

3. SNAIL TRAIL

There's a snail at the bottom of a 10-foot well. Every day the snail climbs up 3 feet. But at night the snail falls back 2 feet. How long does it take the snail to get to the top of the well?

_____

(Hint: Try drawing a picture.)

4. SQUARE DEAL

To complete this square, use the numbers 1 through 9 only once to fill each of the spaces.

Each row, column, and diagonal will add up to a different sum. Some of the boxes are done for you.

1		3
8		4
7		

16

5. TRIANGLE TRICK

Can you add one more triangle to make five triangles in this picture?

6. PAINT PUZZLE!

Imagine that you could paint the cube below and then take it apart. How many of the cubes would not have any paint on them at all?

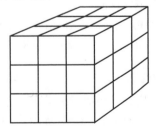

Answers on page 64.

An Assessment Toolkit

Alternative methods of assessment provide a comprehensive profile for each student. As students work on *50+ Super-Fun Math Activities: Grade 5*, here are some ways you might observe and record their work. Alone or in combination, they can provide a quick snapshot that will add to your knowledge of students' development in mathematics. They also give you concrete observations to share with families at reporting time.

FILE CARDS

An alphabetical file system, with a card for each student, provides a handy way to keep notes on students' progress. Choose a few students each day that you plan to observe. Pull their cards, jot down the date and activity, and record comments about their work.

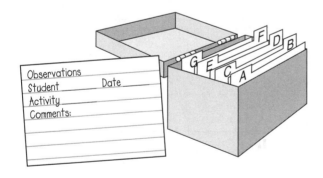

CLIPBOARDS

With a list of students attached to your clipboard, you can easily move about the classroom and jot down observations about their work and their thinking. If you want to focus on a particular skill or competency, you can create a quick checklist and simply check as you observe.

STICKY NOTES

As you circulate while individuals or small groups are working, create a sticky note for students who show particular strengths or areas for your attention and help. Be sure to date the note. The advantage to this technique is that you can move the notes to a record folder to create a profile; you can also cluster students with similar competencies as a reminder for later grouping.

CHECKLISTS AND RUBRICS

On pages 62 and 63, you'll find a few ready-made checklists and a rubric. Feel free to them, or modify them to suit your own needs. Invite students to assess their own work—they are honest and insightful, and you'll have another perspective on their mathematical development!

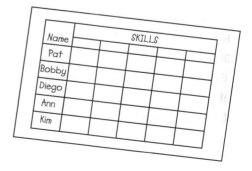

Self-Evaluation Form

ACTIVITY _____

1. The activity was **(HARD EASY)** to complete because _____

_____

_____

2. The part of the activity I did best was _____

_____

_____

3. I could have done a better job if _____

_____

_____

4. The mathematics I used was _____

_____

_____

5. After completing the activity I felt _____

because _____

_____

6. I would rate my work on the activity as **(EXCELLENT GOOD FAIR POOR)**

because _____

_____

50+ Super-Fun Math Activities: Grade 5 © 2010 by Scholastic Inc.

Assessment Checklist

Activity _____ Date _____ Group _____

Students					
MATHEMATICS KNOWLEDGE					
Understands problem or task					
Formulates and carries out a plan					
Explains concepts clearly					
Uses models or tools appropriately					
Makes connections to similar problems					
Can create similar problems					
MATHEMATICAL PROCESSES					
Justifies responses logically					
Listens carefully to others and evaluates information					
Reflects on and explains procedures					
LEARNING DISPOSITIONS					
Tackles difficult tasks					
Perseveres					
Shows confidence in own ability					
Collaborates/shares ideas					

SCORING RUBRIC

3 Fully accomplishes the task

Shows full understanding of the central mathematical idea(s)

Communicates thinking clearly using oral explanation or written, symbolic, or visual means

2 Partially accomplishes the task

Shows partial understanding of the central mathematical idea(s)

Written or oral explanation partially communicates thinking, but may be incomplete, misdirected, or not clearly presented

1 Does not accomplish the task

Shows little or no grasp of the central mathematical idea(s)

Recorded work or oral explanation is fragmented and not understandable

Answers to Problems and More

1. 18 three-sail ships

2. You would have to drive 1010 more miles before the odometer reads 13031.

3. The answer is always 1089.

4. The next five numbers are 55, 89, 144, 233, 377. To get the next number, add together the two previous numbers.

5. The solution is to draw lines like this:

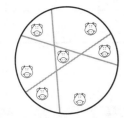

6. Trip 1: The bear and lion cross together. Trip 2: The lion comes back alone with the boat. Trip 3: The ape crosses by itself and stays. Trip 4: The bear takes the boat back to get the lion. Trip 5: The bear and lion cross together.

7. The circles should be filled like this:

8. 18 elephants

PAGE 60

1. The circles and squares should be filled like this:

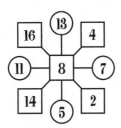

2. The number is 180.

3. It takes the snail 8 days to get to the top of the well. Students' drawings might look like this.

4. The completed square should look like this:

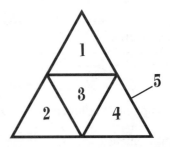

5. By adding the center triangle, students make a total of five triangles in the

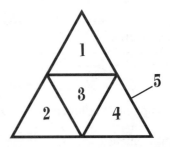

picture.

6. Only one cube would have no paint on it at all: the one in the very center.